Jazz Etude Inspirations

8 PIANO ETUDES

INSPIRED BY THE MASTERS

ISBN 978-1-4584-0357-5

HAL•LEONARD®
CORPORATION
7777 W. BLUEMOUND RD. P.O. BOX 13819 MILWAUKEE, WI 53213

In Australia Contact:
Hal Leonard Australia Pty. Ltd.
4 Lentara Court
Cheltenham, Victoria, 3192 Australia
Email: ausadmin@halleonard.com.au

PERFORMANCE NOTES

JELLY ROLL ME HOME (p.6)
Inspired by Jelly Roll Morton

Ferdinand Joseph LaMothe (1885-1941) better known as **Jelly Roll Morton,** is arguably the first jazz musician. In fact, Morton himself claimed to have invented jazz singlehandedly in 1902! Of Creole origin, Morton began his piano career playing in a brothel in New Orleans at the age of fourteen. As his career progressed, he toured as a soloist and with several vaudeville acts. Many of his compositions, including "Jelly Roll Blues" and "King Porter Stomp", have become standards of the traditional jazz repertoire.

To the Student:
Pedaling is the focal point of this etude. Stride pianists were experts at joining different beats together with the sustain pedal, and this piece challenges the right foot. In the first eight measures, beats one and three should be joined with the pedal to beats two and four; but in the second eight measures, beats two and four need to be linked with beats one and three. Practice this piece without pedal first and add the pedaling once the notes are mastered.

For more, I recommend the following CDs:
Complete Library of Congress Recordings: Jelly Roll Morton (Box Set – Rounder Records, 1938)
Jelly Roll Morton: 1926-1930 (JSP Records – 2000)
Piano Rolls (Nonesuch – 1997; actual piano rolls made in 1924)

> The *Complete Library of Congress Recordings* comprise a first-rate, seven-disc historical record, including both recordings of Morton playing his works and talking about them in interviews with Alan Lomax, his biographer. Morton plays many of his most famous pieces and provides interesting insight into the background and inspiration behind them.

COUNT ON ME (p.9)
Inspired by Count Basie

Count Basie is an original member of piano royalty. Basie (1904-1984), who hails from Kansas City, is most famous for leading a big band that launched the careers of many of the most important jazz artists in history, including Lester Young, Herschel Evans, and Harry "Sweets" Edison. As a piano stylist, Basie is known as a minimalist, providing tasteful filler to complement his big band's raucous outbursts. A nine-time Grammy winner, Basie led his band for nearly fifty years, including stints in which it backed singers like Joe Williams, Ella Fitzgerald, Frank Sinatra, and Tony Bennett.

To the Student:
One of Count Basie's signatures "licks" (memorable musical phrases) is an alternation between playing a high note with his fifth finger, a third with his middle fingers, and a lower note with the thumb (mm. 9-10). This "lick," the main musical motive of "Count on Me," requires *rotation*, the same kind of movement someone's hand/wrist/arm might make when turning a doorknob. Practice blocking each measure by playing all of the notes together as a chord. Then, play the passages as written while moving your fingers as little as possible. Make sure to rotate as much as possible from the forearm rather than the wrist.

For more, I recommend the following CDs:
The Complete Decca Recordings (Decca, 1992)
Count Basie Swings: Joe Williams Sings (Polygram, 1955)
Frankly Basie (Polygram, 1963)

> With the world's swingingest band and America's hippest singer, how could *Count Basie Swings: Joe Williams Sings* be anything less than a monumentally good time? The perfect backing band, Basie's group roars and whispers behind Williams' signature, velvety tone. Standout tracks include "Every Day I Have the Blues" and "Too Close for Comfort."

TEARS FALLING INTO STILL WATER (p.12)
Inspired by Duke Ellington

Edward Kennedy "Duke" Ellington (1899-1974) is a true member of jazz royalty. Originally from Washington, D.C., Ellington is generally considered to be among the greatest composers in American history. Ellington composed over 1,000 pieces and arranged many of them for his big band, which scored numerous hits including *Take the 'A' Train, Satin Doll, Don't Get Around Much Anymore*, and *Prelude to a Kiss*. Known for his impeccable taste and sophisticated palette, Ellington possessed an encyclopedic knowledge of harmony and often married European chord progressions to African American rhythms and forms. A pianist as well as composer, his playing influenced pianists like Thelonious Monk, Jaki Byard, and Bud Powell.

To the Student:
Ellington's music often merges simple melodies with complex harmonies. The challenge for the performer is to allow the melody to sing out without being interrupted or distracted by the rich chords of the arpeggiated accompaniment. Practice the right hand melody alone before adding in the accompanying figures.

For more, I recommend the following CDs:
Piano Reflections (Blue Note, 1953)
Live at Newport (Sony, 1956)
Blues in Orbit (Columbia, 1958)

> The title of *Blues in Orbit* is a good one – on this album, Ellington takes the blues form and spins it around every which way, with unusual treatments, unexpected departures, and creative additions. This concept makes for an album that's simultaneously easy to listen to and dizzyingly sophisticated.

OSCAR'S BOUNCE (p.15)
Inspired by Oscar Peterson

Oscar Peterson (1925-2007) stands among the most celebrated *virtuosi* of jazz piano. Originally from the Montreal area, Peterson began his career with Norman Granz's "Jazz at the Philharmonic" series, where he established a trio with bassist Ray Brown and guitarist Herb Ellis. His more than 200 recordings showcase his spectacular technique in both hands, deeply felt sense of the blues, velvety tone, and elaborate arrangements. Even after a stroke impeded the left side of his body in 1993, Peterson maintained a busy performing and recording schedule.

To the Student:
"Oscar's Bounce" is an exercise in accenting the "and" part of beats two and four, just like Peterson does. When the accents are played properly, their jagged-sounding inflection produces the ebullient rhythmic energy that defines Peterson's style. Make sure that the accents come from the whole arm-forearm-torso apparatus and not just the finger. Watch videos of Peterson and try to mimic the way in which he utilizes his considerable weight to add depth to his sound and intensity to his rhythmic feel.

For more, I recommend the following CDs:
At the Concertbegouw (Verve, 1954)
Night Train (Polygram, 1963)
We Get Requests (Polygram, 1964)

> *Night Train* is an album consisting of short pieces linked by their roots in the blues. Peterson doesn't let loose as he does on some other albums, tending towards simpler, grooving melodies, simply enjoying the rhythmic ecstasy of playing along with highly compatible musicians. *Night Train* shows a confident jazz trio playing at their highest level.

MINOR TYNER (p.18)
Inspired by McCoy Tyner

McCoy Tyner (b.1938), a native of Philadelphia, rose to prominence during his tenure in saxophonist John Coltrane's quartet. Together with Coltrane, Tyner reinvented jazz harmony, bringing "modal music" into prominence. Modal music is music that remains on one chord and scale for long periods of time. Besides his long stint with Coltrane, Tyner has made many memorable albums as a leader, and has recorded on koto, flute, and percussion besides piano. His playing is both angular and visceral, and its intensity conveys his spiritual commitment to music making.

To the Student:
"Quartal voicings," Tyner's signature innovation, form the centerpiece of Minor Tyner. Quartal voicings are chord spacings using only the interval of a fourth. These voicings will place the performer's hands in unusual positions. Because the chords' intervals are so wide, playing them requires use of both hands, meaning that the left hand must maneuver back and forth between bass notes and chords. One good way to practice these types of jumps is to rehearse leaping extra octaves. Move the bass notes down an octave further while playing the chords in the normal position. Also, try practicing these jumps with a blindfold – the results will be rewarding!

For more, I recommend the following CDs:
The Real McCoy (Blue Note, 1967)
Sahara (OJC, 1991)
A Love Supreme (by John Coltrane, Impulse/Verve, 1965)

> Consistently appearing on lists of the greatest albums ever made, *A Love Supreme* is a suite of four pieces about struggling for spiritual enlightenment. These meditations show modal music at its most exciting – rhythmically intense, filled with strident dissonances and potent resolutions, and bursting with ecstatic freedom.

PINEAPPLE WOMAN (p.21)
Inspired by Herbie Hancock

Pianist and composer **Herbie Hancock** (b. 1940), has enjoyed an impressively long and diverse career in jazz, funk, and popular music. Since rising to prominence as the pianist in Miles Davis' storied second quintet, Hancock has pursued a variety of projects merging jazz and popular music. An early exploration, *Head Hunters*, was a pioneering album for the jazz "fusion" genre. It was followed by fusion classics like *Thurst* and *Rockit*. Hancock has recorded with nearly every important artist in the popular music field, from Stevie Wonder to John Mayer to Christina Aguilera. He has won 13 Grammys for his work, including a recent "Album of the Year" for *River: the Joni Letters* in 2008, an album consisting of jazz versions of Joni Mitchell's songs.

To the Student:
"Pineapple Woman" pays tribute to a Hancock piece entitled "Watermelon Man." Listen to "Watermelon Man" (there are versions on *Takin' Off* and *Head Hunters*) to better understand the funky spirit of this music. The main challenge of this piece is to hear and play two simultaneous melodies – the zigzagging, active bassline in the left hand and the slower, soulful melody in the right hand. Even though the bassline is more active than the melody, it should remain at an appropriate volume for an accompaniment. Practice the left hand alone until it feels natural and easy before adding the right hand.

For more, I recommend the following CDs:
Takin' Off (Blue Note, 1962)
Head Hunters (Sony, 1973)
River: The Joni Letters (Verve, 2007)

> From the very first notes of "Chameleon," *Head Hunters* will keep even the most stoic listener tapping their toes. Performed on a mixture of acoustic and electric instruments, *Head Hunters* combines a depth of groove and a harmonic ingenuity that only Hancock could pull off. Not satisfied to merely perform on one or two chords like many other funk artists, Hancock diverts the harmony through fascinating twists and turns while never losing rhythmic vitality.

HAND BATTLE (p.24)
Inspired by Chick Corea

Modern jazz great **Chick Corea** (b. 1941) is known for his unusual harmonic palette, percussive command of the piano, and experimentation with electronic instruments. Many of Corea's recordings combine jazz and rock elements, and his hallmark groups such as *Return to Forever* and *The Elektric Band* revolutionized jazz "fusion" music. Corea is also known for playing the "keytar," a keyboard that has a built in synthesizer and is held with a strap like a guitar.

To the Student:
Two-handed percussiveness, a signature of Corea's music, is central to this piece. Many of the rhythms are intentionally tricky and require mastery of the relationship between downbeats and offbeats. Tap each section accurately before attempting to play it on the piano. Practice not only with each hand tapping its own part but also with both hands tapping the right-hand part and both feet tapping the left-hand part.

For more, I recommend the following CDs:
Now He Sings, Now He Sobs (Blue Note, 1968)
Return to Forever (ECM, 1972)
My Spanish Heart (Polygram, 1976)

> Revered as one of the greatest trio albums ever produced, *Now He Sings, Now He Sobs* features Czech bassist Miroslav Vitous and legendary drummer Roy Haynes. Corea's darkened harmonic palette becomes an unstoppable creative wave when teamed with the dynamic drumming of the veteran Haynes. Besides standard tunes and original compositions, the album features free improvisations in which the group composes new pieces together on the spot.

REPEAT AFTER ME (p.28)
Inspired by Brad Mehldau

Brad Mehldau (b. 1970), the youngest pianist featured in this book, has played a defining role in the current aesthetic of jazz music. A native of Hartford, Connecticut, Mehldau is known for exploring odd meters (not divisible by two or three) and borrowing harmonies and textures from classical composers like Schumann, Schubert, and Brahms. He's also credited with expanding the jazz repertoire to include songs written by rock artists like Radiohead, Nick Drake, and Paul Simon, among others. An innovative composer as well as a pianist, Mehldau became the first jazz musician to hold the *Debs Composer Chair* at Carnegie Hall during the 2010-11 season.

To the Student:
The main challenge of this piece is maintaining the constant repeated notes supporting the melody without allowing them to dominate. Some pianists prefer to play repeated notes with a single finger over and over again, whereas others prefer to switch fingers each time a note repeats. Try both ways to see which you prefer. Either way, remember that the secret to playing fast, clean repeated notes is to let the key come up quickly (not to press it down quickly). Make sure to play this piece on different pianos, because different pianos respond very differently to repeated notes.

For more, I recommend the following CDs:
Art of the Trio, Volume 1 (Warner Bros., 1997)
Largo (Nonesuch, 2002)
Anything Goes (Nonesuch, 2004)

> Put the greatest jazz pianist of his era together with one of the most revered producers from the popular music world and what do you get? *Largo* is the collaboration between Mehldau and Jon Brion, the man behind Fiona Apple, Elliot Smith, Rufus Wainwright and many others. *Largo* features a wide variety of textural experiments, brought together by Brion's shifty moodiness and Mehldau's unique pianistic approach.

Jelly Roll Me Home

Inspired by Jelly Roll Morton

Jeremy Siskind

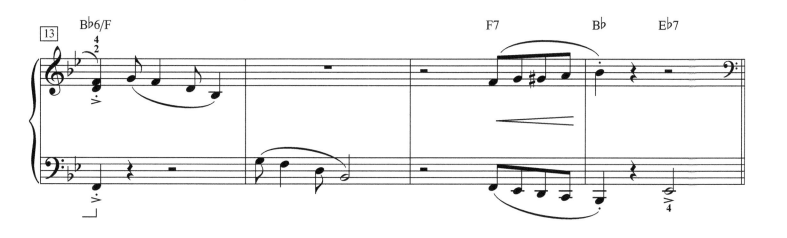

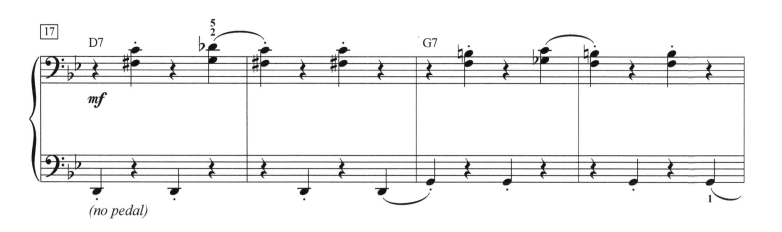

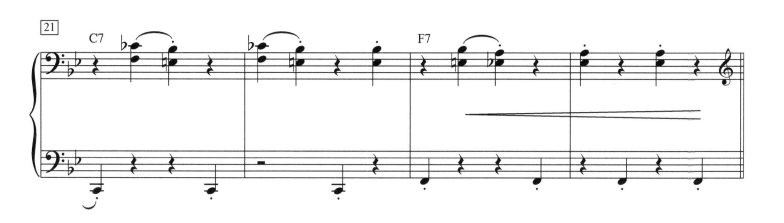

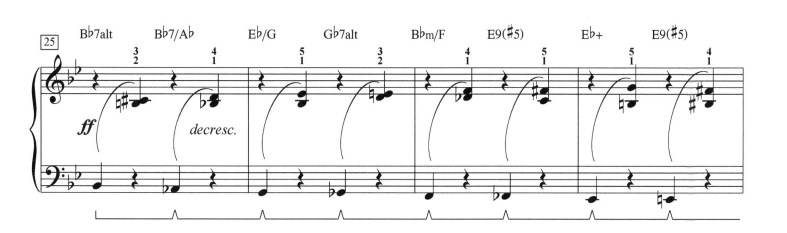

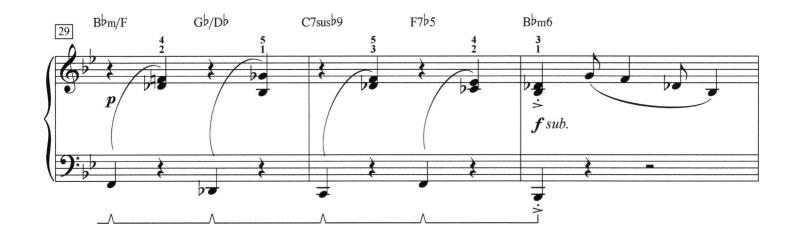

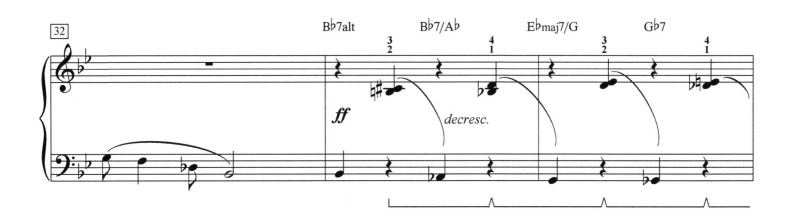

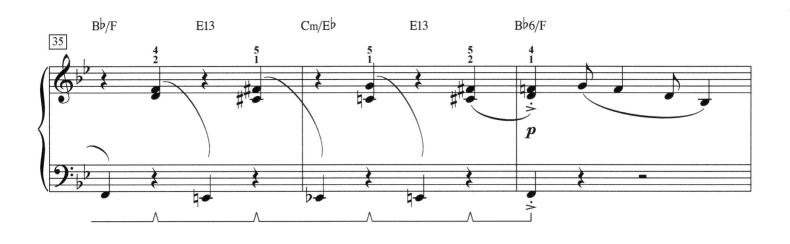

Count On Me

Inspired by Count Basie

Jeremy Siskind

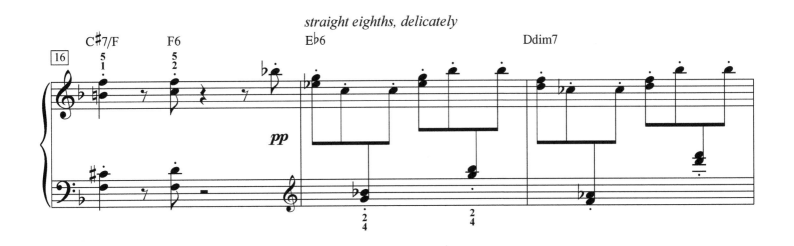

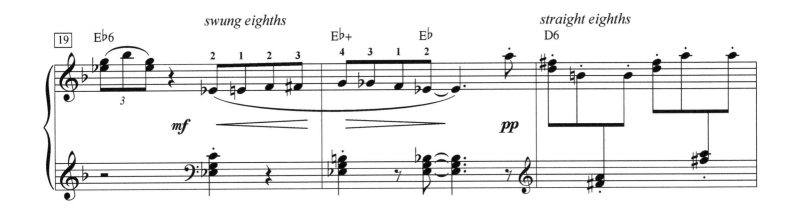

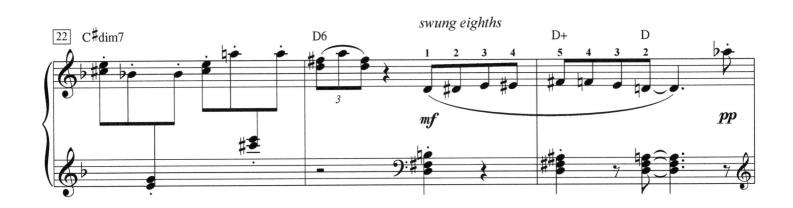

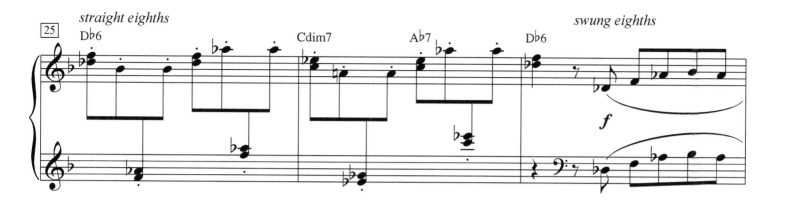

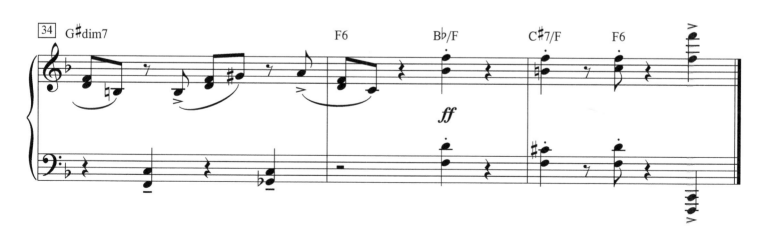

Tears Falling into Still Water

Inspired by Duke Ellington

Jeremy Siskind

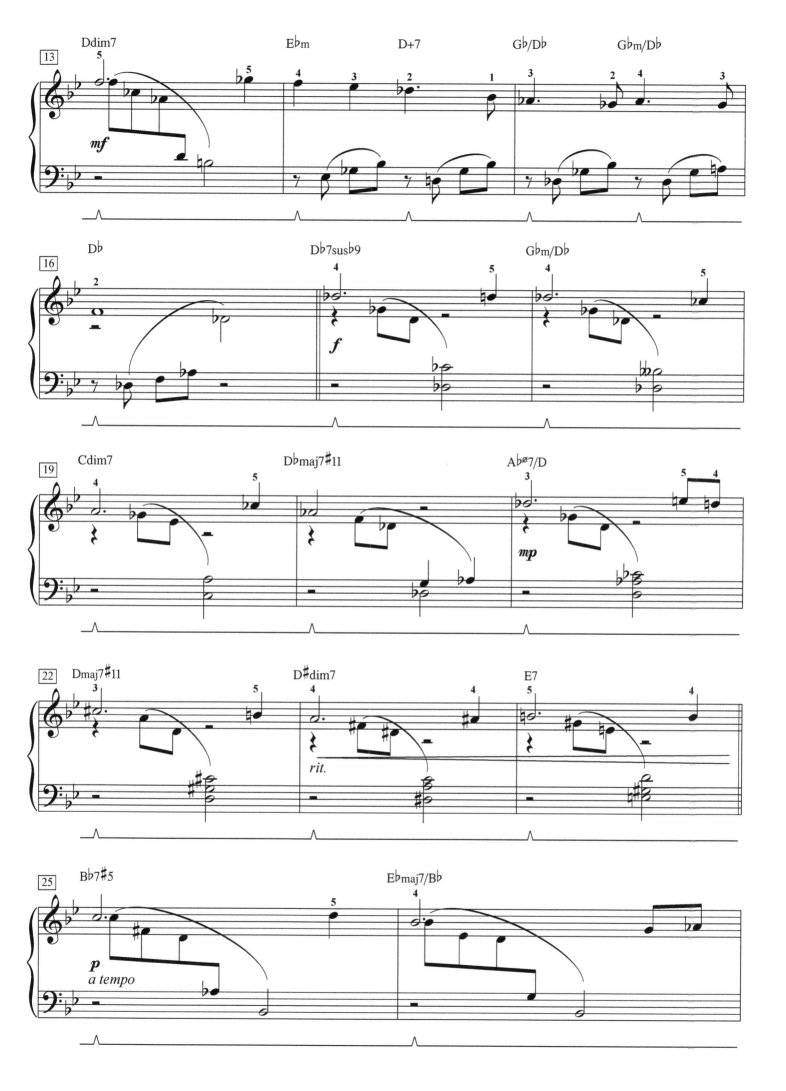

Oscar's Bounce

Inspired by Oscar Peterson

Jeremy Siskind

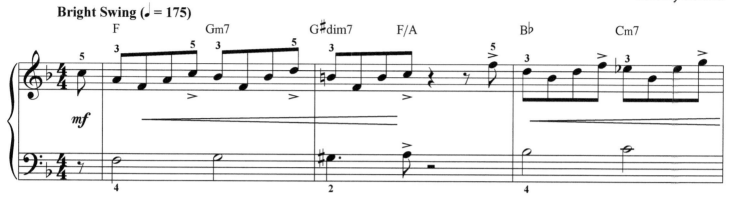

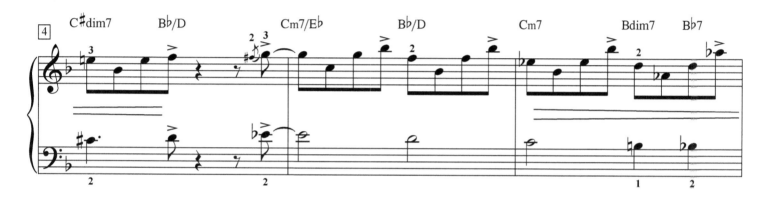

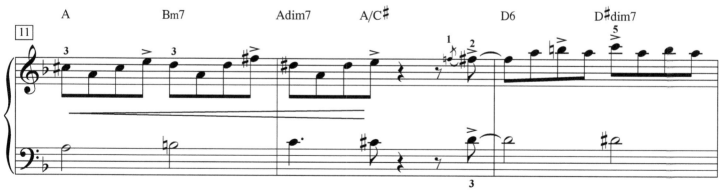

Minor Tyner

Inspired by McCoy Tyner

Jeremy Siskind

Pineapple Woman

Inspired by Herbie Hancock

Jeremy Siskind

Hand Battle

Inspired by Chick Corea

Jeremy Siskind

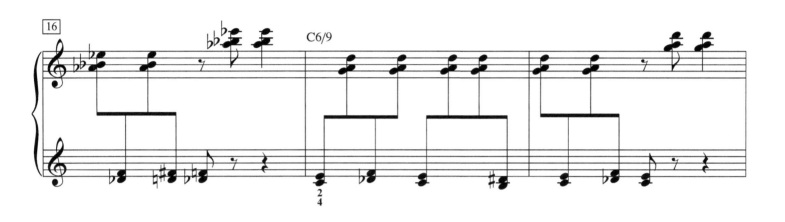

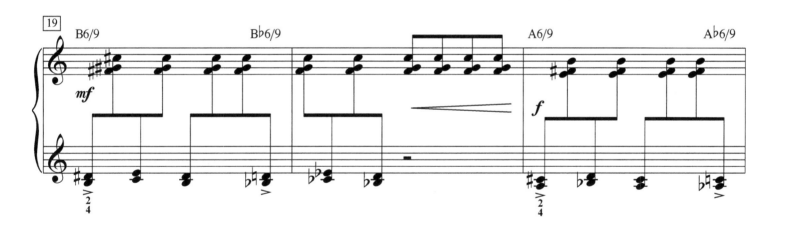

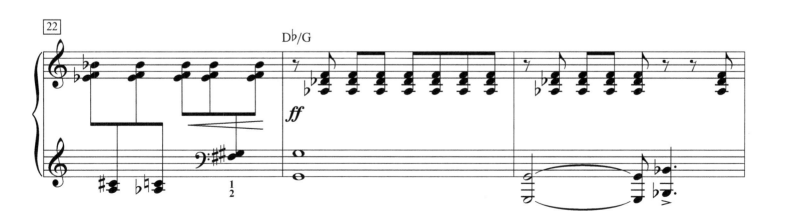

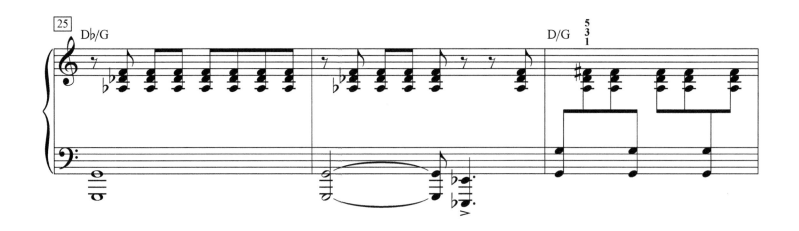

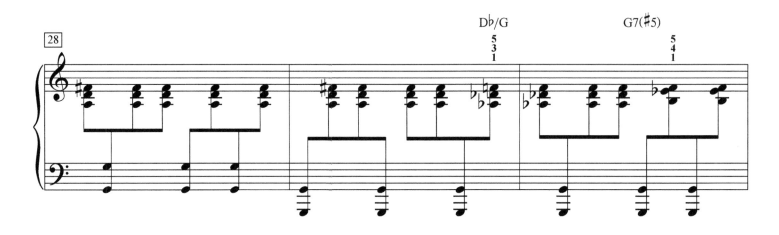

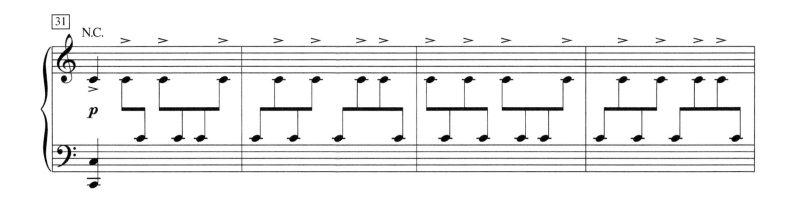

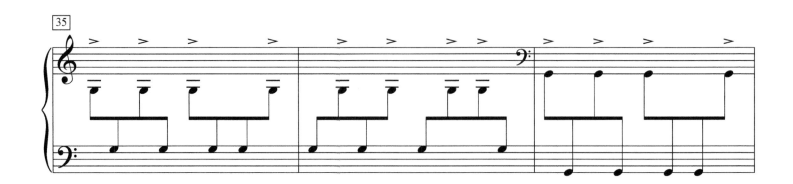

Repeat After Me

Inspired by Brad Mehldau

Jeremy Siskind

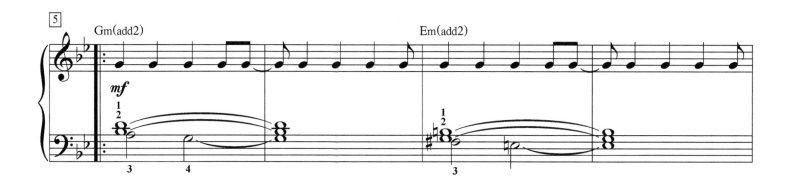

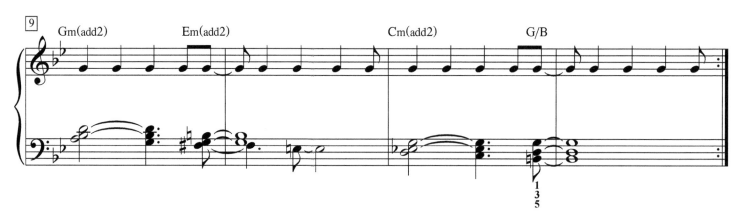

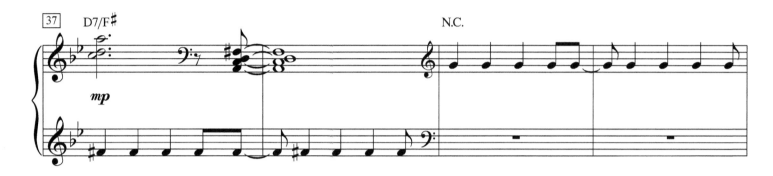

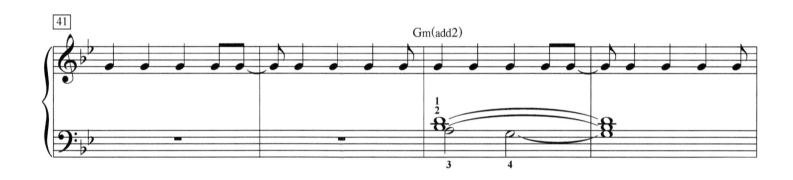

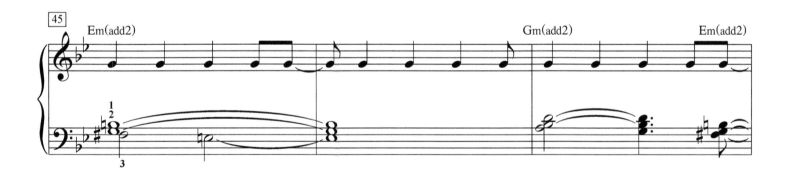

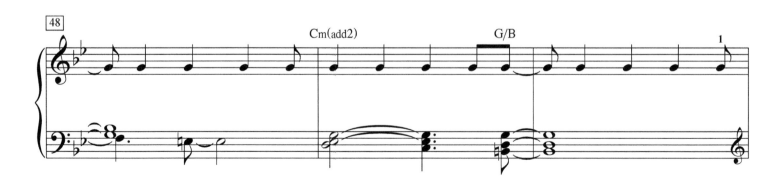

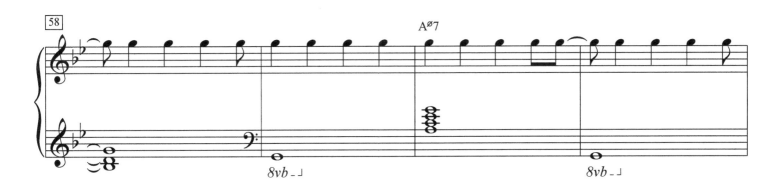

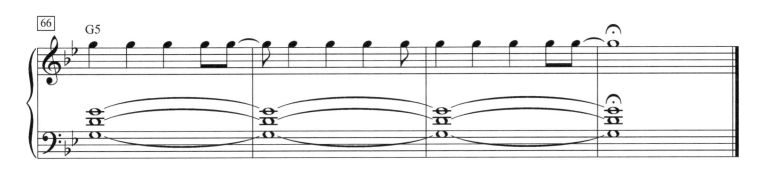

POPULAR SONGS
HAL LEONARD STUDENT PIANO LIBRARY

The **Hal Leonard Student Piano Library** has great songs, and you will find all your favorites here: Disney classics, Broadway and movie favorites, and today's top hits. These graded collections are skillfully and imaginatively arranged for students and pianists at every level, from elementary solos with teacher accompaniments to sophisticated piano solos for the advancing pianist.

Adele
arr. Mona Rejino
Correlates with HLSPL Level 5
00159590......................$12.99

The Beatles
arr. Eugénie Rocherolle
Correlates with HLSPL Level 5
00296649......................$12.99

Irving Berlin Piano Duos
arr. Don Heitler and Jim Lyke
Correlates with HLSPL Level 5
00296838......................$14.99

Broadway Favorites
arr. Phillip Keveren
Correlates with HLSPL Level 4
00279192......................$12.99

Chart Hits
arr. Mona Rejino
Correlates with HLSPL Level 5
00296710......................$8.99

Christmas at the Piano
arr. Lynda Lybeck-Robinson
Correlates with HLSPL Level 4
00298194......................$12.99

Christmas Cheer
arr. Phillip Keveren
Correlates with HLSPL Level 4
00296616......................$8.99

Classic Christmas Favorites
arr. Jennifer & Mike Watts
Correlates with HLSPL Level 5
00129582......................$9.99

Christmas Time Is Here
arr. Eugénie Rocherolle
Correlates with HLSPL Level 5
00296614......................$8.99

Classic Joplin Rags
arr. Fred Kern
Correlates with HLSPL Level 5
00296743......................$9.99

Classical Pop – Lady Gaga Fugue & Other Pop Hits
arr. Giovanni Dettori
Correlates with HLSPL Level 5
00296921......................$12.99

Contemporary Movie Hits
arr. by Carol Klose, Jennifer Linn and Wendy Stevens
Correlates with HLSPL Level 5
00296780......................$8.99

Contemporary Pop Hits
arr. Wendy Stevens
Correlates with HLSPL Level 3
00296836......................$8.99

Cool Pop
arr. Mona Rejino
Correlates with HLSPL Level 5
00360103......................$12.99

Country Favorites
arr. Mona Rejino
Correlates with HLSPL Level 5
00296861......................$9.99

Disney Favorites
arr. Phillip Keveren
Correlates with HLSPL Levels 3/4
00296647......................$10.99

Disney Film Favorites
arr. Mona Rejino
Correlates with HLSPL Level 5
00296809 ....$10.99

Disney Piano Duets
arr. Jennifer & Mike Watts
Correlates with HLSPL Level 5
00113759......................$13.99

Double Agent! Piano Duets
arr. Jeremy Siskind
Correlates with HLSPL Level 5
00121595......................$12.99

Easy Christmas Duets
arr. Mona Rejino & Phillip Keveren
Correlates with HLSPL Levels 3/4
00237139......................$9.99

Easy Disney Duets
arr. Jennifer and Mike Watts
Correlates with HLSPL Level 4
00243727......................$12.99

Four Hands on Broadway
arr. Fred Kern
Correlates with HLSPL Level 5
00146177......................$12.99

Frozen Piano Duets
arr. Mona Rejino
Correlates with HLSPL Levels 3/4
00144294......................$12.99

Hip-Hop for Piano Solo
arr. Logan Evan Thomas
Correlates with HLSPL Level 5
00360950......................$12.99

Jazz Hits for Piano Duet
arr. Jeremy Siskind
Correlates with HLSPL Level 5
00143248......................$12.99

Elton John
arr. Carol Klose
Correlates with HLSPL Level 5
00296721......................$10.99

Joplin Ragtime Duets
arr. Fred Kern
Correlates with HLSPL Level 5
00296771......................$8.99

Movie Blockbusters
arr. Mona Rejino
Correlates with HLSPL Level 5
00232850......................$10.99

The Nutcracker Suite
arr. Lynda Lybeck-Robinson
Correlates with HLSPL Levels 3/4
00147906......................$8.99

Pop Hits for Piano Duet
arr. Jeremy Siskind
Correlates with HLSPL Level 5
00224734......................$12.99

Sing to the King
arr. Phillip Keveren
Correlates with HLSPL Level 5
00296808......................$8.99

Smash Hits
arr. Mona Rejino
Correlates with HLSPL Level 5
00284841......................$10.99

Spooky Halloween Tunes
arr. Fred Kern
Correlates with HLSPL Levels 3/4
00121550......................$9.99

Today's Hits
arr. Mona Rejino
Correlates with HLSPL Level 5
00296646......................$9.99

Top Hits
arr. Jennifer and Mike Watts
Correlates with HLSPL Level 5
00296894......................$10.99

Top Piano Ballads
arr. Jennifer Watts
Correlates with HLSPL Level 5
00197926......................$10.99

Video Game Hits
arr. Mona Rejino
Correlates with HLSPL Level 4
00300310......................$12.99

You Raise Me Up
arr. Deborah Brady
Correlates with HLSPL Level 2/3
00296576......................$7.95

HAL•LEONARD®
7777 W. BLUEMOUND RD. P.O. BOX 13819 MILWAUKEE, WI 53213

Visit our website at www.halleonard.com

Prices, contents and availability subject to change without notice. Prices may vary outside the U.S.